DRUG ADDICTION AN[...]

Drug Use and the Law

WITHDRAWN

DRUG ADDICTION AND RECOVERY

Drug Use and the Law

Michael Centore

SERIES CONSULTANT
SARA BECKER, Ph.D.
Brown University School of Public Health
Warren Alpert Medical School

MASON CREST

Mason Crest
450 Parkway Drive, Suite D
Broomall, PA 19008
www.masoncrest.com

MTM Publishing, Inc.
www.mtmpublishing.com

President: Valerie Tomaselli
Vice President, Book Development: Hilary Poole
Designer: Annemarie Redmond
Copyeditor: Peter Jaskowiak
Editorial Assistant: Andrea St. Aubin

Series ISBN: 978-1-4222-3598-0
Hardback ISBN: 978-1-4222-3602-4
E-Book ISBN: 978-1-4222-8246-5

Library of Congress Cataloging-in-Publication Data
Names: Centore, Michael, 1980- author.
Title: Drugs and the law / by Michael Centore.
Description: Broomall, PA : Mason Crest, 2017. | Series: Drug addiction and
   recovery | Includes bibliographical references and index.
Identifiers: LCCN 2016003949| ISBN 9781422236024 (hardback) | ISBN
   9781422235980 (series) | ISBN 9781422282465 (ebook)
Subjects: LCSH: Drugs—Law and legislation—United States—Juvenile literature. | Drugs
   of abuse—Law and legislation—United States—Juvenile literature.
Classification: LCC KF3885 .C46 2017 | DDC 344.7303/229—dc23
LC record available at http://lccn.loc.gov/2016003949

Printed and bound in the United States of America.

First printing
9 8 7 6 5 4 3 2 1

TABLE OF CONTENTS

Key Icons to Look for:

Words to Understand: These words with their easy-to-understand definitions will increase the reader's understanding of the text, while building vocabulary skills.

Sidebars: This boxed material within the main text allows readers to build knowledge, gain insights, explore possibilities, and broaden their perspectives by weaving together additional information to provide realistic and holistic perspectives.

Research Projects: Readers are pointed toward areas of further inquiry connected to each chapter. Suggestions are provided for projects that encourage deeper research and analysis.

Text-Dependent Questions: These questions send the reader back to the text for more careful attention to the evidence presented there.

Educational Videos: Readers can view videos by scanning our QR codes, providing them with additional educational content to supplement the text. Examples include news coverage, moments in history, speeches, iconic sports moments and much more!

Series Glossary of Key Terms: This back-of-the-book glossary contains terminology used throughout the series. Words found here increase the reader's ability to read and comprehend higher-level books and articles in this field.

SERIES INTRODUCTION

Many adolescents in the United States will experiment with alcohol or other drugs by time they finish high school. According to a 2014 study funded by the National Institute on Drug Abuse, about 27 percent of 8th graders have tried alcohol, 20 percent have tried drugs, and 13 percent have tried cigarettes. By 12th grade, these rates more than double: 66 percent of 12th graders have tried alcohol, 50 percent have tried drugs, and 35 percent have tried cigarettes.

Adolescents who use substances experience an increased risk of a wide range of negative consequences, including physical injury, family conflict, school truancy, legal problems, and sexually transmitted diseases. Higher rates of substance use are also associated with the leading causes of death in this age group: accidents, suicide, and violent crime. Relative to adults, adolescents who experiment with alcohol or other drugs progress more quickly to a full-blown substance use disorder and have more co-occurring mental health problems.

The National Survey on Drug Use and Health (NSDUH) estimated that in 2015 about 1.3 million adolescents between the ages of 12 and 17 (5 percent of adolescents in the United States) met the medical criteria for a substance use disorder. Unfortunately, the vast majority of these

> ## IF YOU NEED HELP NOW . . .
>
> SAMHSA's National Helpline provides referrals for mental-health or substance-use counseling.
> 1-800-662-HELP (4357) or https://findtreatment.samhsa.gov
>
> SAMHSA's National Suicide Prevention Lifeline provides crisis counseling by phone or online, 24-hours-a-day and 7 days a week.
> 1-800-273-TALK (8255) or http://www.suicidepreventionlifeline.org

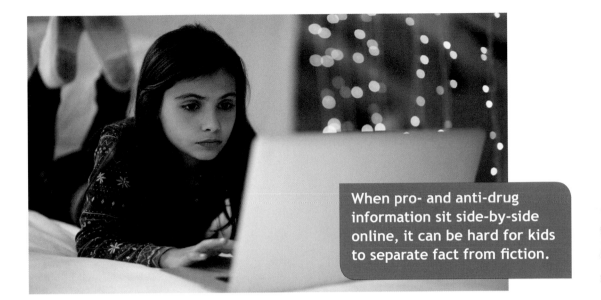

When pro- and anti-drug information sit side-by-side online, it can be hard for kids to separate fact from fiction.

adolescents did not receive treatment. Less than 10 percent of those with a diagnosis received specialty care, leaving 1.2 million adolescents with an unmet need for treatment.

The NSDUH asked the 1.2 million adolescents with untreated substance use disorders why they didn't receive specialty care. Over 95 percent said that they didn't think they needed it. The other 5 percent reported challenges finding quality treatment that was covered by their insurance. Very few treatment providers and agencies offer substance use treatment designed to meet the specific needs of adolescents. Meanwhile, numerous insurance plans have "opted out" of providing coverage for addiction treatment, while others have placed restrictions on what is covered.

Stigma about substance use is another serious problem. We don't call a person with an eating disorder a "food abuser," but we use terms like "drug abuser" to describe individuals with substance use disorders. Even treatment providers often unintentionally use judgmental words, such as describing urine screen results as either "clean" or "dirty." Underlying this language is the idea that a substance use disorder is some kind of moral failing or character flaw, and that people with these disorders deserve blame or punishment for their struggles.

And punish we do. A 2010 report by CASA Columbia found that in the United States, 65 percent of the 2.3 million people in prisons and jails met medical criteria for a substance use disorder, while another 20 percent had histories of substance use disorders, committed their crimes while under the influence of alcohol or drugs, or committed a substance-related crime. Many of these inmates spend decades in prison, but only 11 percent of them receive any treatment during their incarceration. Our society invests significantly more money in punishing individuals with substance use disorders than we do in treating them.

At a basic level, the ways our society approaches drugs and alcohol—declaring a "war on drugs," for example, or telling kids to "Just Say No!"—reflect a misunderstanding about the nature of addiction. The reality is that addiction is a disease that affects all types of people—parents and children, rich and poor, young and old. Substance use disorders stem from a complex interplay of genes, biology, and the environment, much like most physical and mental illnesses.

The way we talk about recovery, using phrases like "kick the habit" or "breaking free," also misses the mark. Substance use disorders are chronic, insidious, and debilitating illnesses. Fortunately, there are a number of effective treatments for substance use disorders. For many patients, however, the road is long and hard. Individuals recovering from substance use disorders can experience horrible withdrawal symptoms, and many will continue to struggle with cravings for alcohol or drugs. It can be a daily struggle to cope with these cravings and stay abstinent. A popular saying at Alcoholics Anonymous (AA) meetings is "one day at a time," because every day of recovery should be respected and celebrated.

There are a lot of incorrect stereotypes about individuals with substance use disorders, and there is a lot of false information about the substances, too. If you do an Internet search on the term "marijuana," for instance, two top hits are a web page by the National Institute on Drug Abuse and a page operated by Weedmaps, a medical and recreational marijuana dispensary. One of these pages publishes scientific information and one publishes pro-marijuana articles. Both pages have a high-quality, professional appearance. If you had never heard of either organization, it would be hard to know which to trust. It can be really difficult for the average person, much less the average teenager, to navigate these waters.

The topics covered in this series were specifically selected to be relevant to teenagers. About half of the volumes cover the types of drugs that they are most likely to hear about or to come in contact with. The other half cover important issues related to alcohol and other drug use (which we refer to as "drug use" in the titles for simplicity). These books cover topics such as the causes of drug use, the influence of drug use on the family, drug use and the legal system, drug use and mental health, and treatment options. Many teens will either have personal experience with these issues or will know someone who does.

This series was written to help young people get the facts about common drugs, substance use disorders, substance-related problems, and recovery. Accurate information can help adolescents to make better decisions. Students who are educated can help each other to better understand the risks and consequences of drug use. Facts also go a long way to reducing the stigma associated with substance use. We tend to fear or avoid things that we don't understand. Knowing the facts can make it easier to support each other. For students who know someone struggling with a substance use disorder, these books can also help them know what to expect. If they are worried about someone, or even about themselves, these books can help to provide some answers and a place to start.

—Sara J. Becker, Ph.D., Assistant Professor (Research), Center for Alcohol and Addictions Studies, Brown University School of Public Health, Assistant Professor (Research), Department of Psychiatry and Human Behavior, Brown University Medical School

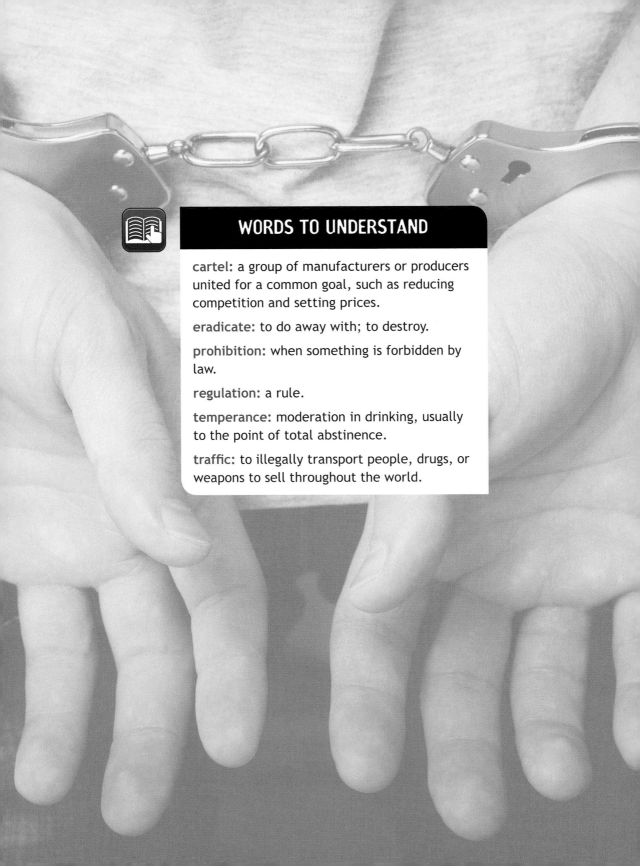

WORDS TO UNDERSTAND

cartel: a group of manufacturers or producers united for a common goal, such as reducing competition and setting prices.

eradicate: to do away with; to destroy.

prohibition: when something is forbidden by law.

regulation: a rule.

temperance: moderation in drinking, usually to the point of total abstinence.

traffic: to illegally transport people, drugs, or weapons to sell throughout the world.

CHAPTER ONE

DRUG LEGISLATION

For centuries, political leaders have tried to protect people from the dangers of substance misuse. They may do this by taxing the substance so that it's more expensive to purchase—cigarettes, for example, are taxed in many countries. Lawmakers might restrict access to the substance to specific group, such as doctors. Or they might ban the substance outright. Each of these kinds of control requires an act of legislation, or legal action. The United States has a unique history of drug legislation, from the unregulated marketplaces of early America to the strict laws of today.

DRUG POLICY IN AMERICA: THE EARLY YEARS

Drug policy was slow to develop in early America, but drug use wasn't. Europeans learned about tobacco from native people in both North and South America. Soon, tobacco was one of the most important products the colonies produced. Rum and beer were incredibly popular drinks in colonial

America, partly because milk and other beverages were difficult to get, and unfiltered water could be dangerous. The settlers not only drank alcohol in large amounts, but they also manufactured it to the point that it became colonial New England's dominant industry.

By the 19th century, America had expanded and its population had skyrocketed. Drinking was still very common, though some people were beginning to worry about its effects on health and society. Leaders such as Doctor Benjamin Rush and the minister Lyman Beecher spoke out against the evils of excessive drinking. Thirteen states passed anti-alcohol laws in the four-year span between 1851 and 1855, though many of these were repealed soon afterwards.

An anti-alcohol drawing from around 1830 by the temperance campaigner George Cruikshank.

Use of other drugs was also a big problem, and early substance-related legislation targeted these other drugs as well. For instance, the Drug Importation Act, passed by Congress in 1848, made sure that the U.S. Customs Service inspected all imported medical drugs to ensure they were not counterfeited, diluted, tampered with, or dangerous. Other state laws made it a crime to mislabel or contaminate prescription or over-the-counter medications.

NEW ADDICTIONS, NEW RESPONSES

In the aftermath of the American Civil War (1861–1865), the American people became aware of the dangers of opiates (drugs made from the opium poppy). Morphine was first developed in the early 19th century. It was used heavily throughout the Civil War to treat all sorts of ailments, from dysentery to malaria, and as a painkiller for soldiers undergoing surgery. At least 200,000 soldiers returned from the war dependent on morphine, bringing the harrowing effects of addiction home to small towns throughout the nation.

Around this time, cocaine, heroin, and other drugs were used in over-the-counter products, often without any rules or regulations whatsoever. For example, the Bayer Company promoted heroin as a way to relieve coughs and induce sleep. Cocaine and heroin were also sold as ways of treating alcoholism. Even soft drinks like Coca-Cola, which were widely advertised as healthy "tonics," contained cocaine. The science behind addiction was not yet understood, but people could clearly see the impacts. As the effects of substance misuse became more recognized, people began to demand that government address the problem.

The first outright ban of drugs came in 1875, when the city of San Francisco outlawed the smoking of opium in opium dens. But the motive for the law had little to do with public health. Instead, it was an anti-immigrant

An opium den around 1900.

measure—smoking opium was a practice associated with Chinese men. The law did not target the sale, trade, or use of opiates in general.

In 1890 the U.S. Congress followed up on this law by placing heavy taxes on opium and morphine. It was the first time the federal government got involved in anti-drug efforts, but it would not be the last. Sixteen years later, the Pure Food and Drug Act was signed by President Theodore Roosevelt. This landmark piece of legislation created the Food and Drug Administration (FDA), a government body responsible for regulating all food and drug products. Products had to be clearly labeled and manufacturers had to be honest about their ingredients. The result was a much safer marketplace for both food and medicine.

THE PROHIBITION ERA

In the early 1900s, the production, transport, and sale of alcoholic beverages was banned in the United States. This new law was called Prohibition. It was spelled out in the Eighteenth Amendment to the Constitution, which was ratified by Congress in 1919. A separate piece of legislation called the Volstead Act was approved to enforce the amendment. The Volstead Act created penalties for people who refused to comply with Prohibition.

The forces behind Prohibition included groups like the Anti-Saloon League and the Woman's Christian Temperance Union—organizations that saw drinking as a root of sinful behavior. There were other inspirations for the temperance movement. There was a strong anti-immigrant aspect, stemming from the fact that Irish, Italian, and German immigrants all came from places with lively drinking cultures. There was also a feminist element, since men who drank were more likely to squander their household finances and physically abuse their wives. Women directly affected by these issues wanted to create safer, better homes by making it harder for their husbands to get alcohol.

Prohibition was somewhat successful in curbing alcohol use, but it also had many negative effects. Among these was a rise in organized crime. Many gangsters illegally obtained alcohol (often from distilleries across the Canadian border) and sold it throughout American cities. By the 1930s, it was clear that Prohibition was failing. Journalists reported

REGULATION VERSUS PROHIBITION

Two terms that come up frequently when talking about substance legislation are regulation and prohibition. Regulation is when a government makes rules about how drugs are made, and when, how, and to whom they can be sold. Prohibition is when the government completely outlaws a particular substance: if someone is caught making, using, or selling it, he or she can be put in jail. Examples of regulated substances in America include alcohol (available to those over age 21), tobacco (available to those over age 18), and Ritalin (available by prescription to those who medically need it). Prohibited drugs include heroin and ecstasy.

AL CAPONE

No doubt the most famous gangster of the Prohibition era was Al Capone. Born in New York but residing in Chicago, Capone was believed to have taken in $100 million a year from organized criminal activities such as bootlegging, prostitution, and gambling.

Al Capone's cell at Eastern State Penitentiary in Pennsylvania. Despite the many violent crimes he committed, it was the crime of tax evasion that sent him to prison.

that 80 percent of congressmen were drinking on the sly. Many wealthy individuals stockpiled alcohol before the law went into effect, while working-class people resorted to making or illegally purchasing alcohol, and were punished if they got caught. These double standards led to the public being fed up with the law. In 1933 the necessary three-fourths of the states approved the Twenty-First Amendment to the Constitution, which repealed the Eighteenth Amendment and ended Prohibition.

But although the Prohibition battle was lost, that didn't mean that the fight for temperance was over. Throughout the 20th century, the U.S. government continued to pass legislation aimed at cracking down on substance use. The Marijuana Tax Act of 1937 levied a tax that made marijuana much more expensive and difficult to get. As with the opium ban in San Francisco, the act was directed against a new immigrant population: Mexicans, who were identified with the drug in southern states. If a Mexican was arrested with marijuana and had not paid the tax, he could be arrested and deported.

THE WAR ON DRUGS

A major shift in American drug policy occurred in 1970, with the passage of the Comprehensive Drug Abuse Prevention and Control Act. This act overhauled many previous drug rules and regulations. It also increased the power of law enforcement to search people for drugs and seize any drugs they found.

The second part of the act, called the Controlled Substances Act (CSA), established five "schedules" of drugs based on how addictive they are and whether they have a real medical use. Schedule I drugs are the most addictive, while Schedule V are the least addictive and may be available "over the counter" without a prescription. A drug's schedule determines how it is regulated—that is, who can manufacture and prescribe it legally. It also determines how someone charged with illegal manufacture, distribution, or possession will be punished.

THE HARRISON NARCOTICS TAX ACT

Some historians trace the origins of the War on Drugs to the Harrison Narcotics Tax Act of 1914. This piece of legislation placed extremely high taxes on opium and cocaine. Although the law did not make the drugs illegal, it made them more difficult to get. Once again, there is reason to suspect that the law was motivated by racist or anti-immigrant views. At the time, opium use was often associated with Chinese immigrants, and cocaine use was often associated with African Americans.

In 1970, President Nixon met with the singer Elvis Presley at the White House. Presley was hoping to be made a "Federal Agent at Large" in the Bureau of Narcotics and Dangerous Drugs. Nixon declined Elvis' offer, but his administration did suggest ideas for how Presley could assist in the anti-drug fight.

Soon after the CSA was passed, President Richard Nixon declared substance misuse to be "public enemy number one" of the United States. So began what has come to be known as the "War on Drugs"—a widespread effort to police, prohibit, and **eradicate** the drug trade, both in America and around the world. In 1973 Nixon established the Drug Enforcement Administration (DEA), a law-enforcement agency tasked with enforcing the laws of the CSA and fighting drug smuggling from abroad. Many criticized Nixon's anti-drug policies as being too harsh, but the reality is that under his watch more funding went to treatment and rehabilitation than to law enforcement.

The drug war continued throughout the 1980s, with President Ronald Reagan signing the Anti-Drug Abuse Act into law in 1986. This established mandatory minimum prison sentences for all drug offenses. Mandatory minimums mean that the length of a sentence is automatically based on the type of drug and how much the person had at the time of arrest. Unfortunately, the Anti-Drug Abuse Act shifted the focus from treatment to punishment.

President Reagan also increased the DEA presence in Latin America, trying to stop drug **trafficking** at the source. To date, the United States has spent over a trillion dollars on anti-drug efforts in Latin America. But instead of stopping the flow of drugs, the efforts have led to an increase in organized crime, violence, and environmental damage as drug **cartels** battle for control of trafficking routes.

The War on Drugs is far from over; the United States spends about $51 billion annually on the fight. Attitudes, however, are changing, as people from all political backgrounds reevaluate the punishment-based system versus alternative approaches such as treatment and prevention. In addition to being significantly cheaper, these alternative methods directly work to fight substance misuse and its negative consequences.

TEXT-DEPENDENT QUESTIONS

1. What was drug policy like in colonial America?
2. Did Prohibition succeed? Why or why not?
3. Which governmental actions led to the "War on Drugs"? What have been some of its policies?

RESEARCH PROJECT

Research a piece of legislation not covered in this chapter that has to do with the control and regulation of substances. Write a summary of the intent behind the law and its actual impact.

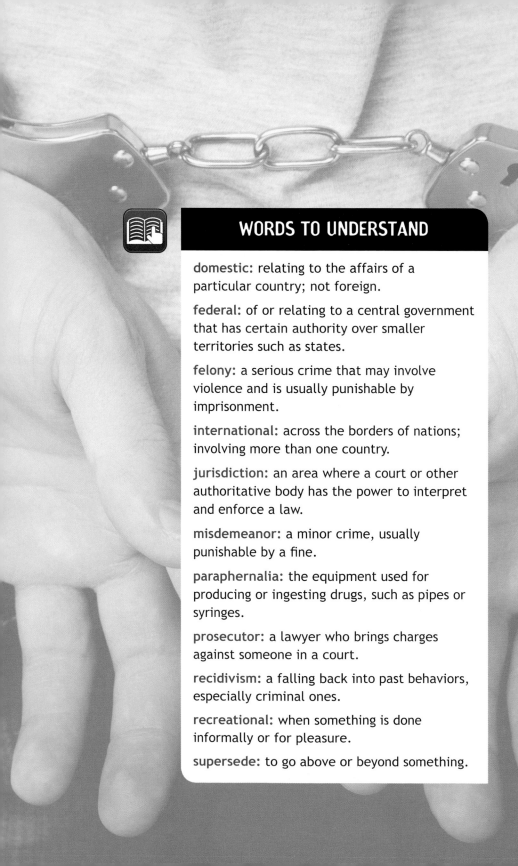

WORDS TO UNDERSTAND

domestic: relating to the affairs of a particular country; not foreign.

federal: of or relating to a central government that has certain authority over smaller territories such as states.

felony: a serious crime that may involve violence and is usually punishable by imprisonment.

international: across the borders of nations; involving more than one country.

jurisdiction: an area where a court or other authoritative body has the power to interpret and enforce a law.

misdemeanor: a minor crime, usually punishable by a fine.

paraphernalia: the equipment used for producing or ingesting drugs, such as pipes or syringes.

prosecutor: a lawyer who brings charges against someone in a court.

recidivism: a falling back into past behaviors, especially criminal ones.

recreational: when something is done informally or for pleasure.

supersede: to go above or beyond something.

CHAPTER TWO

DRUG LAW AND ENFORCEMENT

There is no doubt about it: drug laws can be very complex. Between state and federal regulations, adult and juvenile courts, and **felony** and **misdemeanor** convictions, the system for prosecuting drug offenders can feel like a giant, complicated maze. Making sense of all the codes and statutes between and across state lines could be your life's work. Meanwhile, attitudes toward drug crimes, both in the United States and across the world, are constantly changing.

THE CONTROLLED SUBSTANCES ACT

When President Richard Nixon signed the Controlled Substances Act (CSA) in 1970, America had over 200 drug laws on the books. These were scattered across various pieces of legislation and difficult to understand. As **recreational** drug use rose in the 1960s, many people in the government felt these outdated laws were no longer sufficient. For example, under then-current laws, it was legal to manufacture drugs such as amphetamines and barbiturates, but it was illegal to distribute and use them.

The CSA was designed to be a more thorough regulatory system. It created five separate "schedules" of drugs, which were based on medical use and potential for addiction. The idea was to make it easier to add or remove substances from the list, without having to change the text of an entire law. There are different penalties for crimes associated with each drug schedule: selling a Schedule I drug will land you more time in prison (and heftier fines) than selling a Schedule V drug.

Not everyone agrees on the classifications. For example, marijuana is a Schedule I drug, which means marijuana possession gets the harshest punishment under federal law. Critics of the current schedule argue that marijuana does have medical purposes, is significantly less dangerous than Schedule II drugs like cocaine, and should not be criminalized. Meanwhile, advocates of the current schedule argue that marijuana is dangerous enough to merit Schedule I status.

The Drug Enforcement Association (DEA) is the legal arm that enforces the CSA. It is also the organization that can start the process of changing the substance schedules, or moving a drug from one schedule to another. The

A medical marijuana dispensary in Durango, Colorado. The laws surrounding pot are quite complicated in the sense that they vary greatly by state.

DRUG SCHEDULES IN THE CONTROLLED SUBSTANCES ACT

Schedule I. No medical use, and high potential for abuse; examples include heroin, ecstasy, and bath salts.

Schedule II. Some medical use, and potential for abuse is still strong, though less than Schedule I; examples include cocaine, Vicodin, and Dexedrine.

Schedule III. Medical use, and moderate potential for dependence; examples include codeine (less than 90 milligrams) and ketamine.

Schedule IV. Medical use, and low potential for dependence; examples include Xanax, Ambien, and Valium.

Schedule V. Mostly medical use; examples include Lyrica and certain cough suppressants.

DEA operates on an **international** level when combatting drug imports. It also works closely with state and local police to fight **domestic** drug-related crime.

FEDERAL VERSUS STATE LAWS

The CSA and the DEA are examples of **federal** programs that address drug problems. State governments have their own drug laws, too. A federal law is valid throughout the nation and enforced by the DEA, while a state law only applies to that particular state and is enforced by state and local authorities. It's possible for a suspect to be charged at both the state and federal levels for the same crime.

In some cases, state drug schedules differ from federal DEA recommendations, which makes law enforcement very confusing. Since 2010 a handful of states have changed their laws on marijuana, either making it a Schedule II drug or legalizing its recreational use. These changes go directly against current federal law, under which all marijuana

Inside a "heroin mill" in the Bronx, New York, which was busted by the Drug Enforcement Agency in 2014.

production is illegal. For example, in California it is legal to grow marijuana for medical purposes, while at the federal level it is illegal. Federal law **supersedes** state law in these cases. This means that DEA agents can arrest Californian growers for something they are doing legally under their own state law. Because of the money, time, and effort involved, the DEA has not gone after individuals who adhere to their state's marijuana laws. It has, however, targeted some large-scale growers and dispensaries.

Whether a drug offense is charged as a felony or misdemeanor depends on three major factors. First is the type and amount of the drug involved. In many states, even possessing a small amount of a Schedule I drug is an automatic felony. Second is whether the person possessing the drug was planning to sell or distribute it. Because the intent to sell an illegal substance is taken very seriously by the courts, it is almost always a felony. Police and **prosecutors** have to decide whether someone had the "intent to sell." One thing that comes into play is the amount of a drug that was found. For example, with marijuana, anything over an ounce might be considered "intent to sell." Another consideration is the way the drug is packaged—wrapped in individual plastic bags for easy distribution, for instance—as well as the possession of other items such as drug **paraphernalia** or evidence of communication with customers.

Third, various "aggravating factors" might push an offense to the felony level. Some of these factors include previous arrests for drug offenses; the location of the alleged crime, especially if it's near a school zone or a public park; or possession of a weapon when the alleged crime was committed.

THE COURT SYSTEM

Just as there are both federal and state laws regarding drugs, there are both federal and state courts that deal with drug offenses. If someone smuggles drugs into the United States from abroad or traffics them across state lines, this would be the **jurisdiction** of a federal court, since the crime is not connected to a specific state. Similarly, if a crime is committed on public land, such as a national park, the case will go to federal court. Other crimes go to state courts, which have a broad jurisdiction to hear all types of cases.

A LONG COMMUTE

In July 2015, President Barack Obama commuted (or reduced) the sentences of 46 drug offenders locked away in federal prisons. His reason was that he believed these people had been excessively punished for their crimes, and that, as a nation of "second chances," America should give these people the chance to correct their mistakes. Most of the sentences commuted were handed down in the 1980s, when anti-drug policies emphasized punishment over treatment even more than they do today. Under current laws, these prisoners would have already done their time and been released. Unfortunately, the 46 cases are only a tiny fraction of the total number of people still in jail for whom this is true.

ROCKEFELLER DRUG LAWS

The so-called Rockefeller Drug Laws were named for Governor Nelson Rockefeller of New York, who enacted them in 1973. The laws established minimum sentences of 15 years in prison for selling two ounces, or possessing up to four ounces, of heroin, morphine, cocaine, or marijuana. At the time, the Rockefeller Drug Laws had support from New Yorkers. City leaders saw crime as a greater threat to the health of their neighborhoods than overpolicing.

New York became the state with the toughest drug laws in the United States. Over the next decade, the prison population rose drastically, but crime rates stayed about the same. Critics argued that most of those in jail were arrested for nonviolent offenses—like selling drugs to maintain their own addiction—and that the laws weren't getting to the root of the problem. The laws also received harsh criticism from civil rights advocates, who claimed that they were racist, since they tended to disproportionately punish African Americans and Latinos. In 1979 the marijuana portion of the laws was changed to reduce the minimum sentence. Thirty years later, then-governor of New York David Paterson said, "I can't think of a criminal justice strategy that has been more unsuccessful than the Rockefeller Drug Laws." In April 2009, New York removed all minimum sentences and allowed more offenders the option of treatment.

Although Nelson Rockefeller was considered to be a "liberal" Republican, the drug laws passed under his administration were the harshest in the country at that time.

Most of those that involve individual citizens, such as drug possession, are tried at the state court level.

An alternative to the traditional court system is the drug court system. Drug courts exist at the federal, state, and local levels. In a traditional court, a drug offender is usually charged with a crime and sentenced to prison. In a drug court, the offender may be ordered to attend a treatment program, stay sober, and report to the court for regular check-ups on his sobriety. If the person does not follow through with treatment or fails to stay sober, a jail sentence can be expected. But for those committed to getting healthy, drug courts are an excellent alternative to years of prison.

Research has shown that drug courts are a more effective way of dealing with drug problems than incarceration or treatment alone. Someone who goes through a drug court is more than twice as likely to remain sober and crime-free than someone released from a state prison. This is because lawyers, probation officers, counselors, and treatment specialists work together as a team to reshape the addict's life and reduce the risk of recidivism (landing back in jail after being released). Drug court eligibility guidelines vary by state, though in general only those charged with nonviolent offenses are considered.

TEXT-DEPENDENT QUESTIONS

1. What are the five schedules of substances and how are they defined?
2. What are some major differences between federal and state drug laws?
3. Why do proponents of drug courts maintain that they are a good idea?

RESEARCH PROJECT

Research drug laws for your state, including misdemeanor versus felony charges, minimum incarceration times, and related fines. Compare your state's laws with a neighboring state as well as with federal laws. Create a summary of how the different laws compare, and which laws are the most strict.

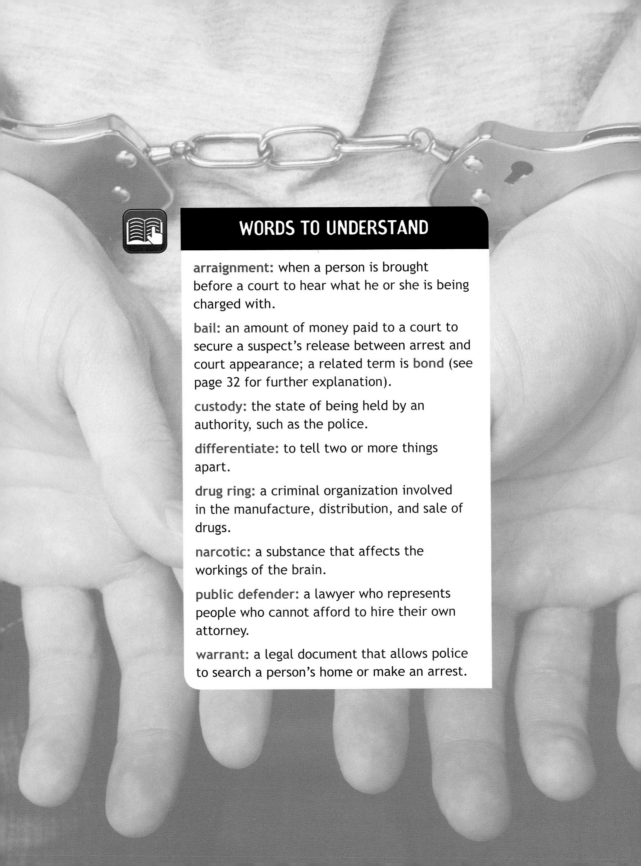

WORDS TO UNDERSTAND

arraignment: when a person is brought before a court to hear what he or she is being charged with.

bail: an amount of money paid to a court to secure a suspect's release between arrest and court appearance; a related term is **bond** (see page 32 for further explanation).

custody: the state of being held by an authority, such as the police.

differentiate: to tell two or more things apart.

drug ring: a criminal organization involved in the manufacture, distribution, and sale of drugs.

narcotic: a substance that affects the workings of the brain.

public defender: a lawyer who represents people who cannot afford to hire their own attorney.

warrant: a legal document that allows police to search a person's home or make an arrest.

CHAPTER THREE

FROM ARREST TO SENTENCING

We often hear about drug-related crimes in the news. Perhaps you've read about someone being arrested for possession of **narcotics**, or seen a story about police infiltrating a "**drug ring**" on television. Maybe it happened to someone you know. But do you know what actually happens *after* a drug arrest is made?

THE ARREST

In the United States, a police officer making an arrest needs to follow a set of standard procedures. These procedures are designed to respect the legal rights of the person being arrested. For example, an arrested person is called a "suspect" until charges are formally filed by a court.

A police officer must have "probable cause" to search someone, which means a strong reason to believe a suspect has drugs—either literally on the suspect's body or in the nearby area, like in a home or vehicle. Maybe the

A state police officer searches a car during a traffic stop in New Hampshire.

officer smelled the odor of marijuana or saw the person drive erratically. Most searches require permission from a judge (a document known as a warrant), but there are exceptions. For example, so-called warrantless searches can occur if the police officer has already arrested the suspect for another crime, if the suspect agrees to the search, or if the officer can see illegal drugs in plain sight.

If drugs are found, the arrest begins the moment the police officer takes the suspect into custody. The officer must read the suspect a text called the Miranda warning to ensure the person understands his or her legal rights.

THE BOOKING PROCESS

After a drug arrest, the officer takes the suspect to the police station or jail for booking. At this time, information about the suspect is recorded to create an official arrest record. Much of this process is done by computer today, but in the past it was written into a book, which is why it's called "booking."

The first step in booking is to enter the suspect's name, date of birth, social security number, and the specific crime into a computer database. This may turn up additional information on the suspect, such as whether the suspect is wanted for other crimes. Next, a "mug shot" is taken of the suspect facing forward and in profile. The pictures help **differentiate** suspects who might have the same name, and show whether a suspect was injured or hurt at the time of his or her arrest. Officers then fingerprint the suspect to further establish identity. In many cases, the suspect will be put in a jail cell to wait for **arraignment**. An officer of the same gender will conduct a full-body search to ensure the suspect isn't hiding any weapons or drugs.

Additional booking procedures might include health screenings (like X-rays or blood tests) to check that the suspect doesn't have any illnesses that will affect other prisoners. Sometimes a sample of the suspect's DNA is taken during the screening, though this usually only happens in the case of very serious crimes.

MIRANDA WARNING

The Miranda warning is a statement that must be read (or recited) to anyone who is put under arrest. Its name comes from an important Supreme Court decision, *Miranda v. State of Arizona* (1966), when the Court ruled that suspects have rights under the Fifth Amendment to the U.S. Constitution. If the police fail to read someone his or her Miranda rights, any confession the person makes will not hold up in court. Here is the full text:

> *You have the right to remain silent. Anything you say or do can and will be used against you in a court of law. You have the right to an attorney. If you cannot afford an attorney, one will be appointed to you. Do you understand these rights as they have been read to you?*

ARRAIGNMENT AND BOND HEARING

For minor drug offenses, the suspect may be able to get out of jail after booking by paying money. This is called posting **bail**. The money is returned to the person once he appears in court at a later date. Bail gives suspects temporary freedom while also discouraging them from skipping their court appearances. **Bonds** are similar to bail in that they offer a suspect temporary freedom. However, bonds are usually a larger amount for more serious crimes and are paid by a bail bond company (see sidebar, "Bondsmen").

More serious offenses do not offer the option of immediate bail. Instead, the suspect must wait for an arraignment hearing. This occurs within 48 hours of the arrest. The suspect is transferred to a holding cell at a courthouse, and then waits (sometimes up to 12 hours) to see a judge. The suspect may have a personal lawyer present, or the court may provide what is known as a **public defender**. Now that the case is formally being filed, the suspect becomes known as a "defendant."

At the arraignment, the judge reads the charges brought against the defendant. The judge will then ask how the defendant pleads: guilty or not guilty. If the defendant pleads guilty, the judge may impose a sentence for the crime right then. There is also a third plea option, which is called "no contest." This is when the defendant neither admits nor denies the offense. If a person pleads no contest to a criminal offense, the plea cannot be used later in a civil lawsuit. Say someone is charged with driving under the influence and has injured someone else. If that person pleads no contest, there will still be a punishment, but the injured person can't use the person's plea of no contest as evidence if he or she sues for damages later.

For serious offenses, a bond hearing often happens at the same time as the arraignment. This is where the judge decides the amount of money the defendant must pay in order to "post bail" or "post bond." The amount is determined by several factors, such as the seriousness of the charges, whether the defendant has been charged with any previous crimes or has any warrants

BONDSMEN

The bail amount given by a judge after an arraignment may be very high. For instance, in Los Angeles County, the standard bail for possessing up to one pound of marijuana with intent to sell is $20,000. Since it's hard to come up with that kind of money all at once, people often use the services of a bail bondsman. A bondsman pays the bail for a standard fee, usually 10 percent of the amount. When the person appears in court, the bondsman gets the money back. If the person doesn't appear in court, the bondsman might send out a bounty hunter—someone trained to catch fugitives.

A bail bond company in Longview, Texas.

out for his or her arrest, and the defendant's standing in the community. A person who has lived a long time in one place, for instance, is more likely to get a lower bail than someone who doesn't have long-term connections to the area. In certain cases the judge will let the defendant go without having to post bail. This is called a "release on recognizance," or "ROR," since it means the court trusts the defendant to return for his or her trial. In the most serious cases, the judge may decide to hold the defendant without bail.

If a defendant doesn't have the money for bail, cannot afford the fees associated with bondsmen, or is not granted an ROR, very few options exist. Such a defendant must often wait in jail until trial. Bail can be set so high—even for relatively minor crimes—that many defendants will plead guilty even when they otherwise wouldn't. A person who feels he or she has been wrongly accused could attempt the difficult task of fighting the case from jail, but court dates are often so far apart and jail is such a difficult place to be that the person might give up and admit guilt. Bail can also be notoriously difficult to post, with courts requiring cash-only payments in exact amounts, acceptable only in a handful of authorized locations. Bondsmen will not take on bails less than a few thousand dollars, leaving many defendants without a payment option. At any given time, there are about 750,000 people in the United States who are locked up in local city and county jails. Of that total, 60 percent have not been convicted of anything—they simply cannot make their bail.

PLEA BARGAINS AND TRIALS

What happens next depends on whether the case is a misdemeanor or a felony. The definitions of misdemeanor and felony differ by state, but an example of a misdemeanor drug charge could be possession of less than an ounce of marijuana, while a felony could be possession of a large amount (say, a pound) with intent to sell.

In a misdemeanor case, the defendant starts with a pretrial conference, where she or he meets with the lawyers and discusses the options for a plea bargain. Here, the defendant may agree to plead guilty to the charge if the prosecutor agrees to reduce the sentence for the crime. A plea bargain keeps the case from going to trial. If the defendant doesn't choose a plea bargain, the case goes to municipal court. If the defendant is convicted, the judge imposes a sentence. For misdemeanors, typical sentences are fines or mandatory hours of community service.

In a felony case, if the defendant pleads "not guilty" at the arraignment, the next step is for the case to go to a preliminary trial, or "prelim." Different states have different laws regarding prelims, and they are not necessarily held in every case. In a prelim, the prosecutor must prove that there is enough evidence for the case to go to trial. There are three possible outcomes: either the case goes to trial, the charges are reduced, or the case is dismissed entirely.

If the case does go to trial, there's a second arraignment at a higher-level court. This is followed by a pretrial conference where the judge works with the prosecution and defense to try and resolve the case through plea bargaining. If necessary, the final step is a trial by jury that results in either a not guilty verdict or, in the case of a guilty verdict, a sentence. Most drug sentences have "mandatory minimum" time lengths. This means that the defendant has to serve a certain amount of time no matter how they behave in jail.

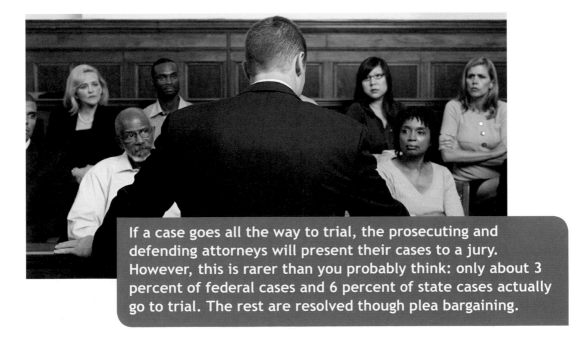

If a case goes all the way to trial, the prosecuting and defending attorneys will present their cases to a jury. However, this is rarer than you probably think: only about 3 percent of federal cases and 6 percent of state cases actually go to trial. The rest are resolved though plea bargaining.

JUVENILE ISSUES

The juvenile justice system is not the same as the adult criminal justice system. A juvenile is usually defined as a person between 10 and either 16 or 18 years of age, depending on the state. Anyone above that age who commits an offense is treated as an adult. In some cases, younger juveniles are treated like adults if the charges are extremely serious.

When dealing with juvenile suspects, police officers can decide not to make an arrest and can instead issue a warning or hold the juvenile in custody until a parent or guardian comes. If the police officer does make an arrest, the case is sent to a juvenile court. In court, a prosecutor reviews the case and decides what to do: dismiss it, settle it informally, or file formal charges.

The San Francisco Juvenile Court and Detention Center. On any given day, there are roughly 70,000 incarcerated juveniles in the United States.

An informal settlement might mean appearing before a judge to hear a lecture, or it might mean taking after-school classes or community service. A formal hearing requires an arraignment. The juvenile may strike a plea bargain, or the judge might force her to pay a fine or attend counseling while the case stays open. More serious cases have what are called adjudicatory hearings, where prosecution and defense lawyers use evidence to argue the case. A big difference between these hearings and adult criminal trials is that juveniles do not have the right to a jury.

At the end of the hearing, the judge makes a ruling and decides a sentence based on what is best for the juvenile. Unlike the adult criminal justice system, the emphasis is placed on rehabilitating the juvenile rather than punishing him. There are roughly 70,000 juveniles in detention in the United States. But courts prefer to send young defendants to counseling or put them on probation. A young defendant might be forced to find a job, do community service, or maintain regular school attendance for a set period of time. Probation usually lasts six months or longer.

TEXT-DEPENDENT QUESTIONS

1. What are the steps of the booking process?
2. How does an arraignment differ from a bond hearing?
3. What are some ways that the juvenile and adult criminal justice systems differ?

RESEARCH PROJECT

Have an adult take you to your local courthouse. Observe the courtroom proceedings from the public gallery for an hour or so—long enough to get a feel for how the process works. Write a brief report detailing what you saw, what the various parties did, and the results of any cases or arraignments you might have witnessed.

WORDS TO UNDERSTAND

controlled substance: a drug that is regulated by the government.

incarceration: being put in prison.

penal: of or relating to punishment or penalties.

probation: when someone is released from jail on the condition that he or she maintains good behavior.

CHAPTER FOUR

PENALTIES, PUNISHMENTS, AND TREATMENTS

Throughout history, those accused of substance misuse have faced serious punishments. The ancient Aztecs believed that alcohol was the root of many evil acts, so they would strangle or beat to death anyone who was found drunk in public. In the 17th century, Czar Michael (Mikhail Fyodorovich Romanov) of Russia condemned to death anyone caught in possession of tobacco. Today in Indonesia, the recommended sentence for drug trafficking is the death penalty. In fact, 32 countries (almost all in Asia or the Middle East) continue to impose the death penalty for drug smuggling. This recurring theme across the world's **penal** systems shows— rightly or wrongly—how seriously societies take substance use.

On average, it costs almost $29,000 to keep one person in federal prison for one year.

MANDATORY MINIMUMS

In the United States, there is a wide range of penalties for drug offenses that differ from state to state. Possession of a **controlled substance** in a small quantity is known as simple possession. It comes with a fine and, in some cases, a jail sentence. The fine may be anywhere from less than $100 to well over $1,000. Depending on the state, the jail sentence can be as short as 15 days or as long as several years. More serious offenses are possession with the intent to sell, the sale of drug paraphernalia, and the cultivation (or growth or production) of drugs. These offenses carry heftier fines and prison sentences.

As noted in chapter one, in 1986 the federal government under Ronald Reagan established a policy of mandatory minimum sentences for drug crimes. Many state legislatures adopted this policy, too. With mandatory minimums, the type of drug and amount found at the time of arrest automatically determine the length of the sentence. For example, being convicted of possessing 1 gram or more of LSD triggers a mandatory sentence of five years. The mandatory minimum is the absolute lowest sentence a judge can give.

However, there are "sentencing guidelines" that give judges a bit more leeway in determining punishment. By taking into account the person's criminal history, whether he or she takes responsibility for the crime, and other factors, the judge may reduce the sentence. But in order to even be considered for sentencing guidelines instead of a mandatory minimum, the accused must qualify for a "safety valve." A safety valve is either a federal or state law that allows courts to give an offender less time in prison if the offender meets certain special requirements. At the federal level, the safety value is a five-item test that assesses the seriousness of the crime—and the person must pass all five items. These are (1) no one was harmed during the offense, (2) the person has little or no history of criminal convictions, (3) the person did not use violence or a gun, (4) the person was not a leader or organizer of the offense, and (5) the person told the prosecutor all he knows about the offense. The only other way to be considered is called "substantial assistance." This is when the accused provides information to help police capture other drug offenders. The decision to grant "substantial assistance" is usually made by the prosecutor and not the judge, and some have argued that it puts too much power in the hands of the prosecutor to determine the final charge.

Mandatory minimums have drawn considerable criticism over the years. At the top of the list is how they have swelled the number of people in jail. The federal prison population in 2015 was eight times what it was in the 1980s, when the laws were first enacted. Fifty percent of inmates in federal prisons are there for specific drug-related offenses, and drugs are implicated in another 30 percent of cases. Many of the offenses were nonviolent, meaning that no one was hurt or injured during the crime. This system costs the government a great deal, and the data suggest that it doesn't reduce the crime rate or the availability of illegal drugs.

Leaders of different political backgrounds have pushed for reforming the system. The Fair Sentencing Act of 2010 got rid of the five-year mandatory minimum for simple possession of crack cocaine. In 2015 an updated version of a piece of legislation called the Smarter Sentencing Act was introduced in Congress. The bill proposes to reduce mandatory minimums for nonviolent drug offenses and allows judges greater freedom in handing down sentences.

TREATMENT VERSUS INCARCERATION

Drug-related criminal offenses like possession, sales, and trafficking are just part of the way that drugs inspire crime. Alcohol or drug use is implicated in 80 percent of offenses leading to incarceration in the United States. Addiction can have such a powerful grip on the brain that users might do things to get the drug that they wouldn't usually do, like stealing or

A NEW APPROACH

After dealing with four overdose deaths in a three-month span in early 2015, the city of Gloucester, Massachusetts, introduced a radical new approach to dealing with opioid addiction. Leonard Campanello, the police chief in the town, announced that those who turned themselves into the police—even if they were acutely intoxicated or had drug paraphernalia on them—would no longer be arrested. Instead, they would be directly referred to treatment. Police staff would have volunteer "angels" on hand—often people who had a history of substance use and recovery—to escort the individuals to a detox facility. There, they could receive Narcan, a drug used to combat opioid overdoses, which would be paid for by money seized from drug dealers. Data from the first nine months of the program indicated that local drug-related crimes dropped by 23 percent.

Although it's an idyllic town in many ways, Gloucester, Massachusetts, has struggled with the same addiction problems that face most towns in America.

prostitution. Substance use can also cause people to make poor decisions, like getting behind the wheel while intoxicated, which can result in offenses like vehicular manslaughter. When high, some users can become violent and abusive, possibly leading to acts of assault or destruction of property. About 60 percent of all individuals who are arrested test positive for alcohol or drug use at the time of arrest, and nearly 50 percent of all jail or prison inmates meet criteria for a substance use disorder. Yet less than 20 percent of inmates receive substance use treatment from a trained professional.

For this reason, many health professionals advocate treatment in place of **incarceration**, or at least as an element of incarceration. Treatment costs significantly less than incarceration. A 2012 research study published in the journal *Crime & Delinquency* found that if just 10 percent of eligible offenders

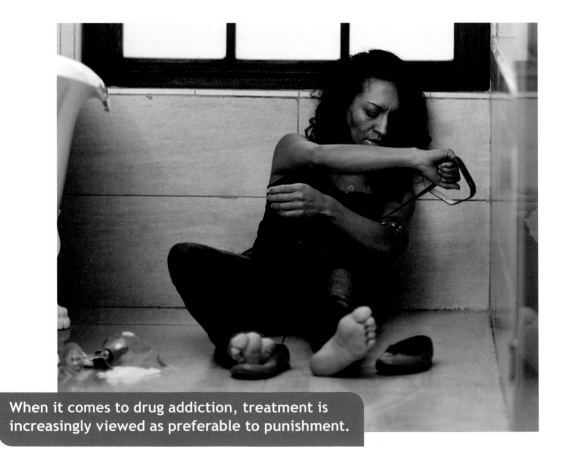

When it comes to drug addiction, treatment is increasingly viewed as preferable to punishment.

were sent to community-based treatment programs instead of prison, the criminal justice system would save $4.8 billion relative to current practices.

As the system currently works, many offenders fall back into old habits of use and dependence after they are released. Having a felony conviction makes it hard to get a job, secure housing, and qualify for government assistance. Ironically, this can lead to more crime and, in some cases, a return to jail. By helping offenders to find positive alternatives to drug use, treatment has the potential to reduce drug use and reduce arrests for drug-related crimes.

There are several ways that the criminal justice system can involve treatment. A court might insist on it as part of a probation program. Drug courts (discussed in chapter three) are another method; here, judges order offenders to attend treatment programs instead of serving a jail sentence. Finally, prisons themselves could improve their efforts to provide more comprehensive treatment programs and work with drug offenders directly. This would change the prison model from one of punishment to rehabilitation, giving people the tools they need to correct past mistakes and reenter society.

JUVENILE ISSUES

Treatment is especially preferable to punishment in juvenile cases. Research suggests that kids who are suspended or expelled from school for substance use issues are more likely to end up in trouble with the law. One type of punishment leads to another, creating more problems at an earlier age. Those who are arrested have a harder time finishing their education, creating a viscous cycle: young offenders fall behind in their studies, making it difficult to find gainful employment, which can result in more drug use and drug-related crime. This is a good argument for focusing on treatment and rehabilitation early on, as soon as substance misuse issues are detected.

ALTERNATIVE SENTENCES

There are other forms of punishment for drug-related crimes besides strict prison sentences. "Indeterminate sentences" are when state legislatures set minimum and/or maximum sentence lengths, but let prison officials determine when to release an offender within those guidelines. This is an incentive for offenders to display good behavior so that they might be released early. On the other

Alternative sentences often have regular drug testing as part of their requirements.

hand, it allows officials to keep those who might need more time for rehabilitation before returning to the community.

A judge also has the ability to delay a prison sentence, in which case the sentence is said to be "suspended." This is also called being "on probation." The offender must meet certain conditions to remain on probation, like obeying all laws (even minor ones like traffic violations), staying sober (and taking drug and alcohol tests to prove it), and reporting regularly to a probation officer.

There are also many "alternative sentences" for lower-level offenders, such as doing weekend jail time. A "house arrest" is when a person must stay at home and wear an electronic monitor to track his or her movements. The person may be allowed to go to work or medical appointments, but otherwise travel is severely limited.

When juvenile offenders are arrested, they face a different court system than adults. Since adolescents are still developing, juvenile courts typically focus on changing the youth's behavior rather than just managing an addiction. Juvenile courts also offer a wider range of social services and, whenever possible, look to treat the entire family and not just the individual. The end goal is to give young people the skills they need to lead healthy and productive lives without turning to substances.

TEXT-DEPENDENT QUESTIONS

1. What are mandatory minimum sentences and how are they determined?
2. What is the difference between treatment and incarceration, and why do many addiction specialists encourage treatment?
3. How do juvenile and adult court systems differ?

RESEARCH PROJECT

Select a drug from the schedule of substances. Research mandatory minimum sentences for at least three types of offenses, such as possession, trafficking, and importation, in at least three different states. Make a chart showing how the sentences differ and how they are the same.

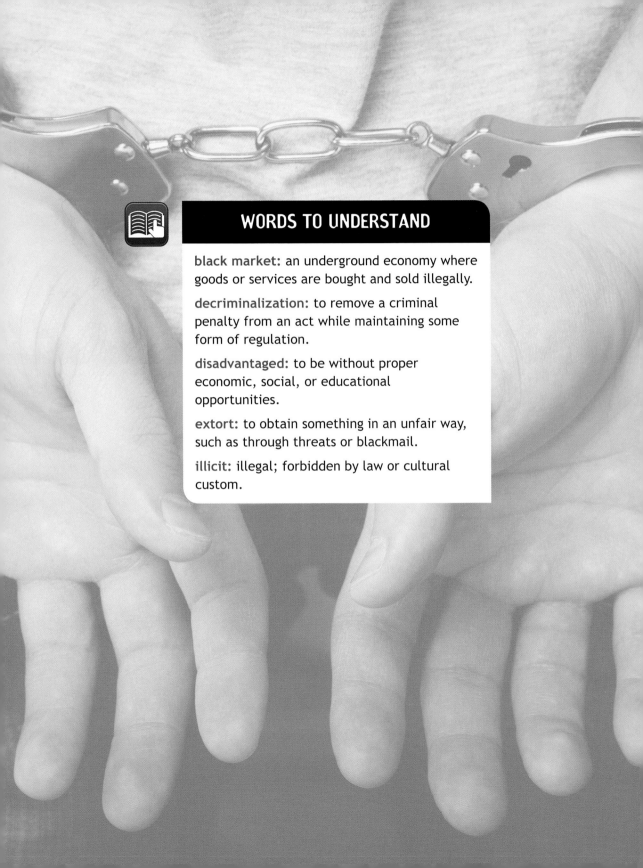

WORDS TO UNDERSTAND

black market: an underground economy where goods or services are bought and sold illegally.

decriminalization: to remove a criminal penalty from an act while maintaining some form of regulation.

disadvantaged: to be without proper economic, social, or educational opportunities.

extort: to obtain something in an unfair way, such as through threats or blackmail.

illicit: illegal; forbidden by law or cultural custom.

CHAPTER FIVE

DRUGS AND INTERNATIONAL LAW

The worldwide market for **illicit** substances is huge—it's worth some $352 billion annually! The illegal drug trade affects the lives of millions of people, and not just those involved directly in buying and selling. Global economies, the health and safety of communities, and the strength of governments are all impacted. Different countries around the world have different drug regulation policies to try to combat this influence. Some take a more lenient approach, believing legalization cuts down on **black market** crime, while others are extremely strict, hoping harsh punishments will stop people from using.

TRAFFICKING

It is estimated that over 200 million people, or about 5 percent of the world's population, use illegal drugs each year. Heroin, cocaine, marijuana, and amphetamines are the main substances of choice. The production, distribution, and sale of these substances involves millions of people from all walks of life. It's estimated that some 4 million rural farmers are involved in the growth of opium for heroin and coca plants for cocaine. These farmers often live in poverty, and growing illicit drugs is the only way they can make a living for their families. Meanwhile, drug dealers in urban areas may be making thousands of dollars a day selling drugs on the street. Linking those two groups are smugglers, who employ all sorts of techniques to transport drugs, from flying them across borders to hiding them in their bodies. At the top of the chain are drug lords who oversee the entire operation. Central America, West Africa, and Afghanistan are the world's primary drug-producing regions.

An officer of the Colombian Police tests evidence as part of a major marijuana bust in Bogotá in 2013.

Officials find drugs that were smuggled inside a spare tire.

The drug trade destabilizes regions in many different ways. One of the most drastic problems is the growth of organized crime. As drug cartels fight to protect their trade routes from authorities, they often resort to murder, bribery, and violent acts of intimidation. They may also fight with each other for control over a trade route, endangering the lives of innocent civilians caught in the line of fire. Many drug cartels don't hesitate

OPIUM PRODUCTION

The two worldwide centers for opium production are known as the Golden Crescent and the Golden Triangle. The Golden Crescent includes parts of Pakistan, Afghanistan, and Iran in western Asia, while the Golden Triangle shares parts of Burma, Laos, and Thailand in Southeast Asia.

Members of the U.S. Agency for International Development speak with an Afghan farmer in a cucumber field near the village of Haji Nikal, Afghanistan, in 2012. The team helps identify farmers who are interested in programs designed to assist them in making a living without growing opiates or marijuana.

to threaten or murder police officers or politicians who try to stop the drug trade. Some gangs recruit children to act as "mules," or low-level smugglers, to bring drugs across the border. These children may be forced to swallow bags of drugs. Not only does this expose children to extreme danger, but it also increases their own risk of addiction.

In some countries, particularly in West Africa, profits from the drug trade can be more than a nation's entire income. This means that cartels can become "substitutes for the state," turning them into "narco-states" ruled entirely by the drug trade. In narco-states, cartels control elections, employ their own police forces, and hold banks hostage, all with the goal of maintaining power. They may **extort** farmers who do not want to cultivate drug crops or politicians with anti-drug views. Political corruption becomes widespread, as officials are threatened into supporting the cartels.

Another issue is that drug cartels are often the only employment available in **disadvantaged** areas. Cartels provide jobs and protection from rival gangs. Some even help with social programs. For example, the Colombian drug lord Pablo Escobar worked hard to cultivate a "Robin Hood" image, using a portion of his earnings to build hospitals and finance sports stadiums—even though he was involved in hundreds, probably thousands, of murders. The sad truth is that cartels control the life of many drug-producing nations, whether the people want it or not. One of the most powerful arguments against hard drug use is exactly this: money that people in rich countries spend on drugs supports an industry that causes the suffering of many people in developing countries.

DECRIMINALIZATION

The "War on Drugs" declared by the United States failed to curb the demand for substances worldwide. As a result, many nations are looking for different strategies to fight drug-related crime. At the top of the list of possible solutions is the **decriminalization** of certain drugs. This is when governments reduce the penalties for possession of a substance. Offenders may be fined and put in treatment programs, but they are not jailed and do not have a criminal record. Decriminalization is different from legalization, where there are no penalties whatsoever.

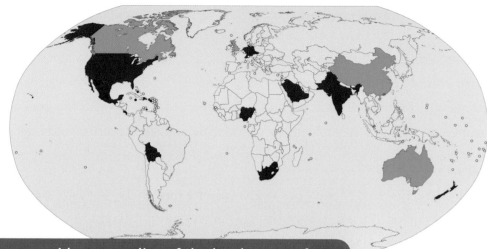

This map provides a sampling of the legal status of cocaine in certain countries as of 2014. Red means illegal, yellow means decriminalized, light blue means legal for medical use only, and dark blue means legal.

Fans of decriminalization point out that Prohibition didn't end alcohol use, and drug prohibition hasn't stopped people from using, either. In fact, the demand for substances inspires more criminal activity—both on the supply side (that is, the producers and distributors) and the demand side (the users). Decriminalization would help remove the stigma of addiction and encourage people to seek treatment. The end result, proponents argue, would be a safer environment for users to address their problems. With fewer addictions, demand for drugs would fall, reducing crime and improving public health.

Opponents of decriminalization say it won't be so easy. The black market would not be totally wiped out unless *all* drugs were legalized and regulated—and even then, a separate black market might spring up to sell drugs at lower costs. Cartels would likely move on to other areas, such as agriculture, to keep themselves in power. Opponents also argue that criminalization keeps the public safe by preventing people—and especially children—from using substances. Addicts would still need money to get decriminalized drugs, and crime might still be committed by people under the influence.

POLICIES AROUND THE WORLD

Drug policies around the world range from very lenient to very strict. Among the more lenient nations are Portugal, Switzerland, and Uruguay. Portugal decriminalized all drugs in 2001 after experiencing high rates of heroin addiction. Today the country has the lowest drug usage rate in the European Union. Portugal's policy provides treatment, rehabilitation, and needle-exchange programs, through which addicts are supplied with clean needles to stop the spread of disease. Needle exchange can be part of a broader treatment plan, ensuring the addict's health as she or he is weaned

BLOOD AVOCADOS

The state of Michoacán in Mexico is an example of how cartels control many aspects of local life—not just drugs. Avocados are Michoacán's largest export. Recently, a cartel called the Caballeros Templarios (Knights Templar) has cornered the avocado trade, forcing farmers to pay "protection fees." They also take over plantations and packing plants, controlling the entire process from growth to distribution, just like they would with illicit drugs.

The avocado trade is so lucrative because Mexico's neighbor to the north, the United States, consumes over $1 billion of the pitted fruit each year. Since there are few growing areas in the United States, avocados must be imported from countries such as Mexico. Americans worried about funding drug cartels should eat domestically produced avocados whenever possible, and avoid buying them out of season when they would have to be imported.

off of the substance. Switzerland has followed a similar program since the 1980s, significantly reducing the spread of HIV/AIDS and the number of overdose deaths. In Uruguay, the legalization of marijuana in 2013 freed the nation's authorities to pursue cocaine and heroin distribution networks. Because citizens can now buy marijuana directly from the government, drug traffickers have seen their influence decline.

On the opposite end of the spectrum, some countries around the world have notoriously strict drug laws. In the year 2013 alone, China executed 2,400 people, many for drug-trafficking offenses. Smuggling less than 1 kilogram of heroin (or less than 50 grams of marijuana or cocaine) is grounds for the death penalty. In Singapore, any person caught leaving a "drug establishment" where substances are known to be used can expect a full police search without a warrant. Convicted heroin traffickers may be subject to execution. Iranian authorities resort to ancient punishments like public flogging (where a person is whipped in plain sight of others) for possession or use of marijuana. Officials of these governments say such policies are the best way to keep their countries safe from drugs, while critics claim they threaten basic human rights and are not proven to reduce drug use.

SAFE INJECTION ROOMS

Safe injection rooms are places where addicts can go to get clean needles for injecting drugs. Nurses are on staff to supervise the process, watch over the health of the user, and get appropriate medical care if something is seriously wrong. Staff members may help users find housing and treatment. Critics say these rooms condone drug use. However, those who go to safe rooms are much more likely to seek out detox services. Safe rooms also prevent the spread of hepatitis and HIV, which are very expensive to treat, and reduce the threat of overdose deaths.

Cannabis activists on the streets of Auckland, New Zealand. As of 2015, marijuana was still illegal there.

TEXT-DEPENDENT QUESTIONS

1. How does the illicit drug trade negatively impact the lives of people in drug-producing countries?
2. How is decriminalization different from legalization? What are the arguments for decriminalization? What are the arguments against it?
3. What is the difference between addressing drug use as a health issue and addressing it as a criminal issue?

RESEARCH PROJECT

Select a country from around the world and research how it handles drug possession, trafficking, and other offenses, and whether it sees addiction as a health or criminal problem. Make a "T-chart" comparing and contrasting how policies differ from those of your own country.

FURTHER READING

BOOKS AND ARTICLES

Alexander, Michelle. *The New Jim Crow: Mass Incarceration in the Age of Colorblindness*. New York: The New Press, 2010.

Hari, Johann. *Chasing the Scream: The First and Last Days of the War on Drugs*. New York: Bloomsbury, 2015.

Maté, Gabor. *In the Realm of Hungry Ghosts: Close Encounters with Addiction*. Berkeley, CA: North Atlantic Books, 2010.

Miller, Gary J. *Drugs and the Law: Detection, Recognition, and Investigation*. 4th ed. Charlottesville, VA: LexisNexis, 2014.

"The Wars Don't Work." *The Economist*, May 2, 2015. http://www.economist.com/news/leaders/21650112-one-war-drugs-ends-another-starting-it-will-be-failure-too-wars-dont-work.

ONLINE

Drug Policy Alliance (DPA). http://www.drugpolicy.org/about-drug-policy-alliance.

FindLaw. "Drug Charges." http://criminal.findlaw.com/criminal-charges/drug-charges.html.

Mann, Brian. "The Drug Laws That Changed How We Punish." National Public Radio, *Morning Edition*, February 14, 2013. http://www.npr.org/2013/02/14/171822608/the-drug-laws-that-changed-how-we-punish.

U.S. Drug Enforcement Administration (DEA). http://www.dea.gov/index.shtml.

EDUCATIONAL VIDEOS

Access these videos with your smartphone or use the URLs below to find them online.

"The Devastating Effects of Mandatory Minimum Sentences." RT America. "Many critics believe the Anti-Drug Abuse Act of 1986 has directly and unfairly targeted minorities and believe reformation is overdue." https://youtu.be/c5L5hJqBeW0

"So What Can We Learn From Portugal?," Versus. A debate about the impact of decriminalization of drugs in Portugal. https://youtu.be/jJMmzcwQ8pQ

"Drug Court: The Beginning," All Rise. "An eye-opening look back at the origins of Drug Court, the most successful response to addiction in American history." https://youtu.be/GDiJj9i4Uws

"Families of Victims Of the Drug War Speak Out," Subliminally. "A film to explain why families around the world are campaigning for reform of international drug laws." https://youtu.be/NaQmDqv2ptc

"TRNN Debate: Decriminalization vs. Legalization," The Real News. "Two leading experts on marijuana policy debate whether marijuana decriminalization can end the racial disparity in drug-related arrests." https://youtu.be/GW3nsHS_Erk

SERIES GLOSSARY

abstention: actively choosing to not do something.

acute: something that is intense but lasts a short time.

alienation: a sense of isolation or detachment from a larger group.

alleviate: to lessen or relieve.

binge: doing something to excess.

carcinogenic: something that causes cancer.

chronic: ongoing or recurring.

cognitive: having to do with thought.

compulsion: a desire that is very hard or even impossible to resist.

controlled substance: a drug that is regulated by the government.

coping mechanism: a behavior a person learns or develops in order to manage stress.

craving: a very strong desire for something.

decriminalized: something that is not technically legal but is no longer subject to prosecution.

depressant: a substance that slows particular bodily functions.

detoxify: to remove toxic substances (such as drugs or alcohol) from the body.

ecosystem: a community of living things interacting with their environment.

environment: one's physical, cultural, and social surroundings.

genes: units of inheritance that are passed from parent to child and contain information about specific traits and characteristics.

hallucinate: seeing things that aren't there.

hyperconscious: to be intensely aware of something.

illicit: illegal; forbidden by law or cultural custom.

inhibit: to limit or hold back.

interfamilial: between and among members of a family.

metabolize: the ability of a living organism to chemically change compounds.

neurotransmitter: a chemical substance in the brain.

paraphernalia: the equipment used for producing or ingesting drugs, such as pipes or syringes.

physiological: relating to the way an organism functions.

placebo: a medication that has no physical effect and is used to test whether new drugs actually work.

predisposition: to be more inclined or likely to do something.

prohibition: when something is forbidden by law.

recidivism: a falling back into past behaviors, especially criminal ones.

recreation: something done for fun or enjoyment.

risk factors: behaviors, traits, or influences that make a person vulnerable to something.

sobriety: the state of refraining from alcohol or drugs.

social learning: a way that people learn behaviors by watching other people.

stimulant: a class of drug that speeds up bodily functions.

stressor: any event, thought, experience, or biological or chemical function that causes a person to feel stress.

synthetic: made by people, often to replicate something that occurs in nature.

tolerance: the state of needing more of a particular substance to achieve the same effect.

traffic: to illegally transport people, drugs, or weapons to sell throughout the world.

withdrawal: the physical and psychological effects that occur when a person with a use disorder suddenly stops using substances.

INDEX

ABOUT THE AUTHOR

Michael Centore is a writer and editor. He has helped produce many titles for a variety of publishers, including memoirs, cookbooks, and educational materials, among others. He has authored several previous volumes for Mason Crest, including titles in the Major Nations in a Global World and North American Natural Resources series. His essays have appeared in the *Los Angeles Review of Books, Killing the Buddha, Mockingbird*, and other print- and web-based publications. He lives in Connecticut.

ABOUT THE ADVISOR

Sara Becker, Ph.D. is a clinical researcher and licensed clinical psychologist specializing in the treatment of adolescents with substance use disorders. She is an Assistant Professor (Research) in the Center for Alcohol and Addictions Studies at the Brown School of Public Health and the Evaluation Director of the New England Addiction Technology Transfer Center. Dr. Becker received her Ph.D. in Clinical Psychology from Duke University and completed her clinical residency at Harvard Medical School's McLean Hospital. She joined the Center for Alcohol and Addictions Studies as a postdoctoral fellow and transitioned to the faculty in 2011. Dr. Becker directs a program of research funded by the National Institute on Drug Abuse that explores novel ways to improve the treatment of adolescents with substance use disorders. She has authored over 30 peer-reviewed publications and book chapters and serves on the Editorial Board of the *Journal of Substance Abuse Treatment*.

PHOTO CREDITS